Dear Lesley

We're glad the Africa "travel bug" has bitten you!

It brought you to aergre at Ukutula. Many thanks for all your enthusiasm and help on the project.

with appreciation

Willi and Gill

On *Safari*

Denny Allen
Peter Joyce

SUNBIRD
PUBLISHERS

2 4 6 8 10 9 7 5 3 1
First Published 2006
Sunbird Publishers (Pty) Ltd
P O Box 6836, Roggebaai, 8012 Cape Town, South Africa

www.sunbirdpublishers.co.za

Registration number: 4850177827
Copyright © 2006 published edition: Sunbird Publishers
Copyright © 2006 text: Peter Joyce
Copyright © 2006 photographs: **Denny Allen** with the exception of:
Nigel Dennis pages 10 (top right), 43, 90 (left and bottom right), 97, 100 (bottom left), 101
(top left), 102 (top right), 103, 104, 105, 106 (all), 107 (top left and bottom right) and back cover;
Wendy Dennis page 70 (bottom right); **Image Collection/MuseuMAfrica** pages 6 and 7;
Mike Myers/Wilderness Safaris pages 9 (top right), 108 (bottom left), 109 (bottom right)
and dustjacket (front flap).

Publisher Natanya Mulholland
Editor Sean Fraser
Designer Mandy McKay
Production Manager Andrew de Kock

Reproduction by Unifoto (Pty) Ltd, Cape Town
Printed and bound by Tien Wah Press (Pte) Ltd, Singapore

All rights reserved. No part of this publication may be reproduced, stored in a retrieval system
or transmitted, in any form or by any means, electronic, mechanical, photocopying, recording
or otherwise, without the prior written permission of the copyright owner(s).

ISBN 1 919 93847 8

TITLE PAGE *Sunset on safari – newly arrived guests at the Kruger National Park's Bateleur
bushveld camp survey the wilderness.*

LEFT *Lion at rest: the Lowveld is home to about 1 500 of these majestic carnivores.*

ABOVE *Southern Africa's elephant herds are thriving; close encounters are a common experience.*

OPPOSITE *A female waterbuck. As the name suggests, these antelope are found near rivers.*

Contents

LEFT *Leopard are quite at home in the branches of a tree. This is a mainly nocturnal hunter, solitary, and rarely seen. Its tawny yellow body, spotted with black rosettes, enables it to blend, virtually undetected, into its bushveld surrounds.*

The Wilderness

Not too long ago, up to about the middle of the nineteenth century, the broad grassland plains of South Africa's northern interior were among Planet Earth's greatest treasure houses of wildlife. Vast herds of springbok, zebra, wildebeest and other grazing animals roamed the sunlit spaces, unhindered by farmlands and fences, free to follow their ancient migratory paths, their numbers limited only by their attendant predators, by periodical drought, and by the rather modest needs of the local peoples.

Then came the Dutch-speaking colonists of the Great Trek and their succeeding kinfolk to parcel up the land and to plunder the game resources. In due course, they were joined by the professional hunter with his large-bore gun and his addiction to the killing sport.

For the most part, these men – farmer and 'sportsman' – hunted not for food or commercial gain, but for sheer entertainment: it was the tally that mattered to them, the number of dead animals left on the veld after an exhilarating day in the wilderness. Nevertheless, for all this disdain for profit, it is reckoned that more than two million hides had been exported to Europe by 1880. Countless other carcasses were left for the scavengers and the bleaching African sun. Clearly, someone had to rescue the region's priceless heritage.

ABOVE *Paul Kruger, president of the Transvaal and deeply conscious of his young republic's dwindling natural heritage.*

Birth of a park

The task fell to Paul Kruger and his Transvaal republican government, who were deeply conscious of their country's dwindling natural assets and who, in the 1890s, set aside as permanent sanctuaries two stretches of countryside beyond the mountains towards the east. One was soon abandoned (following an outbreak of stock disease), but the other, which lay between the high escarpment and the border with Portuguese East Africa (now Mozambique), proved a striking success. It was known as the Sabi and eventually, when more land had been added, became the Kruger, South Africa's first national park.

These were groundbreaking moves, the first chapter in the subcontinent's long and sometimes inspiring story of conservation. And they weren't too costly, either: the area selected was part of the spacious eastern coastal plain, low-lying, ferociously hot, humid, fever-ridden, and home to a scatter of hardy locals and a huge concourse of wild animals. It was also something of a hunter's hell.

ABOVE *Death of an elephant. Nineteenth-century commercial and 'sporting' hunters devastated the great herds of the interior. Eventually, strict conservation laws were enforced and, in southern Africa, the animal has flourished.*

Most poisonous of the front-fanged snakes are the mambas and cobras. Anti-venom serum is widely available.

Use common sense and take appropriate precautions, especially if you're on a self-guided trip. On conducted safaris, the ranger will know the ropes, and his or her instructions should be followed to the letter.

Finally, a word about bush etiquette for independent travellers on safari in southern Africa.

Remember that parks and reserves are intended to preserve the environment, its wildlife and the inter-relationships among the myriad species – animals, birds, insects, plants, micro-organisms – that maintain the fragile cycle of life. Leave your vehicle only at designated spots: picnic and viewing points, water holes if it's safe to do so (notices will tell you). Light fires only at barbecue and camp sites; consign cigarette stubs to the ashtray, especially in the winter months; camp fires should be doused after a meal, the embers covered in earth before you depart. Leave the camp spotless; don't litter the countryside; keep a plastic bag for all that rubbish that accumulates on a journey.

Stick to the roads; don't try to take short cuts or make exploratory forays into the trackless veld. To do so is to

ABOVE *The African buffalo – placid-looking but dangerous when cornered. Herds have evolved a laager-like group defensive system.*

ABOVE *An international ban on the ivory trade and careful wildlife management have enabled elephants to flourish rather too well. If the numbers aren't controlled, they can do enormous damage; a full-grown individual will consume up to 300 kilograms of vegetation a day.*

damage the environment. More important, if you do stray from the beaten path, you might break down, and if your cellphone can't pick up a signal you'll be stranded without any guarantee of early rescue.

Don't feed the animals. If a baboon – or any other species – becomes used to human handouts it will be considered a nuisance and in all likelihood will have to be put down.

Viewing game

As we say, approach big game with caution, with as little noise and movement as possible, and preferably from a downwind direction. This applies especially, but not exclusively, to those on wilderness walks and hikes. Never cut an animal off from its group or its line of retreat, and never ever cut a hippo off from its water source. Enter observation hides as quietly as you can and stay under cover for at least half an hour – in your own interests.

Patience is the key to good game-viewing; it is usually more profitable to play the waiting game, notably at water holes, than to drive around in search of sightings. You may not see much at first, though there's always something to be observed – a warthog family perhaps; a kingfisher; a mongoose – and sooner or later the larger, more charismatic animals will arrive.

Try to learn, beforehand, something of the habits and habitats of the wildlife, especially those forms you're particularly interested in seeing. Invest in a good large-scale physical map of the area and look for species in the place where they are most likely to feed, drink and find cover. Animals tend to lie up in the hotter hours, so best viewing times are early morning and late afternoon. The chances of spotting lions are better just after dawn; elephant, giraffe, rhino, buffalo and other large game are usually at their most visible in the hour before sunset.

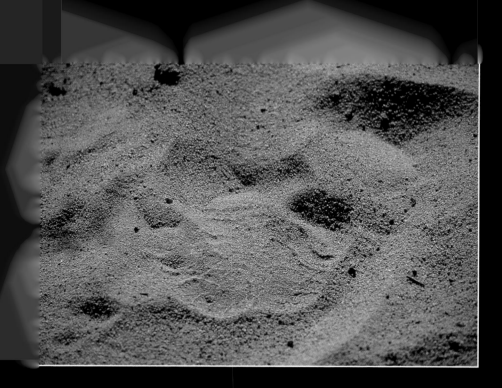

THESE PAGES The tracks of Africa's Big Five...

LEFT AND BOTTOM LEFT Spoor and foot of the white rhinoceros, which is found in savanna bushveld, rarely in grassland. Males weigh up to 2 000 kilograms, females somewhat less. This is a grazing animal, with a wide mouth and a preference for the short grasses, in contrast to its smaller black cousin, which has the pointed mouth of the browser.

BELOW Footprint of the African elephant, largest of the world's land mammals: it reaches a mass of some 7 000 kilograms and a shoulder height of 3.4 metres. This is a resident of the savanna and woodlands of the Lowveld sanctuaries; adult females produce a single calf every three to four years; the gestation period is 22 months; the calf is weaned after 18 to 24 months.

OPPOSITE, TOP LEFT Leopard paw print. This nocturnal big cat is the most elusive of all the major predators, found in many habitats but prefers broken, wooded country. It hunts by stealth, using cover with masterly skill and immense patience.

OPPOSITE, BOTTOM LEFT Hoofprint of the African buffalo, known for its bulk, its enormous strength, and its ability to face down dangerous carnivores, even lions.

OPPOSITE, TOP RIGHT AND BOTTOM RIGHT Spoor and feet of the lion, the continent's supreme predator and the bushveld's prime drawcard. Habitat varies depending on the availability of medium-sized and large prey; females give birth to one to four cubs any time of the year.

The Hunters

Among the rarest and arguably smartest of the Lowveld's big carnivores is the African wild dog. And, in terms of group dynamics, it is also perhaps the most complex. Allen Reich, a keen observer who watched a Kruger hunting pack in action, later committed his wonder and admiration to paper, noting that the animal that had led the hunt, the front runner, stood back from the carcass. All the other dogs were 'eating peacefully, save for the subordinate male. He had made the kill; he had trotted back to the others; he had let them taste the blood on his mouth, and he had led them back. Now he waited for what, to our human minds, was rightfully his. He eventually managed a few scraps … What a remarkable creature!'

That incident illustrates how sophisticated the wild dog's social organisation is. Each individual's seniority within the pack, its place in the hunt and its rights to the spoils are subtly and precisely defined. The order changes as time goes by – as cubs are born, adults grow old and dominance is challenged. But group survival remains the overriding imperative; all is given over to the wellbeing of the pack as a whole.

ABOVE *Mainly nocturnal, hyaenas have great stamina and are always ready for a long chase.*

ABOVE *A rare glimpse of the nocturnal leopard is a memorable highlight of a Sabi Sand safari. Most of the private lodges lay on darkness drives for the guests; spotlights mounted on four-wheel drives show the way. The Lowveld is home to about a thousand of these big cats.*

More often seen and more resilient have been the lions of the bushveld: Kruger is haven to some 1 500 of these impressive animals, largest of the land predators. They range throughout the region, though tend to be more numerous in those grassland areas, in the central and southern parts, that are favoured by antelope and other large herbivores.

Lions are the only members of the cat family that live in groups, prides of perhaps half a dozen members (sometimes more) who cooperate with a remarkable degree of mutual understanding during the hunt. The females do most of the work; the male tends towards indolence, though when called on he can put on a remarkable show of power. He is quite able to bring down a full-grown wildebeest with one swipe of his massive paw. And don't be deceived by his lazy manner: if stirred, he will come to life with terrifying suddenness, and he can cover 100 metres in under six seconds.

Understandably, lions have no natural enemies. On the other hand, mortality within the prides is high: cubs die in times of drought, and lean seasons expose the under-nourished animals to parasite-borne diseases. Adults are open to injury in their quest for prey – from the horns of a buck, for example; from the hefty kick of a giraffe and, oddly enough, from sharp contact with the needle-sharp quills of a porcupine which may spread infection. Fights for dominance also take their toll; a wounded lion all too often becomes a dead lion. The numbers, too, are kept down by infanticide. Backbone of the pride is the female and her same-age cubs; young males move off, often in sibling pairs, and roam for a few years before challenging an established leader for control of a family. If they win this sometimes deadly confrontation, they will kill the existing cubs – a harsh but necessary dynamic designed to secure the integrity of the victor's genes.

A powerful animal indeed. But not, surprisingly, an ecologically dominant one: contrary to general perception, it isn't this great carnivore that keeps the numbers of prey species in check; lions have been competing with antelope, zebra and other prey species for millions of years, and the herbivores have developed their own systems of defence (based on their acute senses, their speed and agility), and it is their presence and availability that determines the survival or otherwise of the predators.

Quite different in habit and habitat is the lion's distant cousin, the leopard. Shy, solitary, secretive, this handsome big cat is the ultimate survivor of the animal kingdom, versatile in its skills, hugely adaptable, able to fit comfortably into pretty well any kind of environment. The species, a nocturnal hunter, is found everywhere from the southern tip of Africa northwards and across parts of Asia to the east, and although urban sprawl and human cultivation have restricted both its presence and its movements, it still manages to turn up in some unlikely places (on the fringes of Johannesburg, for instance). In the Lowveld, it spends the daylight hours hiding away in dense bush or among the jumble of a rocky outcrop. Occasionally, very occasionally, it will brave the open ground,

ABOVE Wildebeest make up a large portion of the lion's diet. Other favourites include zebra, giraffe and buffalo.

but remains difficult to spot – its tawny body, which is dappled with black rosettes, blending extremely well with the surrounds. The leopard's favourite prey are small to medium-sized antelope, which it often drags up to a 'larder' in the high branches of a tree. That said, however, it isn't too fussy about its diet, taking anything from a tiny field mouse right up to a baby giraffe.

Far less successful is the third of the big cats, the cheetah – fastest and, when on the move, lyrically loveliest of all mammals. This delicate creature, with its sinuously streamlined body, its deep keel-like chest and long legs, is superbly built for the explosive chase over open ground, its tail and supple spine giving it perfect balance.

The last of the Lowveld's charismatic carnivores is the spotted hyaena, an animal much maligned in myth and fable as the very embodiment of evil, believed variously to be the harbinger of death and the packhorse of witches. Much of the superstition and folklore derives from the sounds it makes, a weird cacophony of whoops, shrieks, cackles and giggles that speak of madness. Even among the fairly well-informed, the image of the hyaena is of a kind of cowardly body-snatcher, a stealthy cemetery-squad scavenger that creeps through the darkness to feed on the kills of other, braver creatures.

Nothing could be further from the truth, however. While the hyaena does indeed scavenge (as do most carnivores), it is also a redoubtable hunter, strong, self-reliant, clever and opportunistic, taking whatever presents itself. The focal point of the female-dominated hyaena community is the den, which serves as a secure hideaway for the cubs while the adults are out looking for food, and as a gathering place where itinerant male members can maintain contact with the clan, establish their status and learn about feeding prospects. Like the wild dog, the species hunts cooperatively, in anything up to 40-strong groups; and resourcefully too: a pack of hyaenas can sometimes rob even lions of their kill,

ABOVE Lions at rest often look nonchalant but appearances are deceptive. Never leave your vehicle in 'undesignated' areas.

harassing and mobbing the pride until the cats eventually retire. The hyaenas then get to work on the carcass, crushing even the biggest of bones (for the rich marrow that these contain) with their extremely tough teeth and immensely powerful jaws.

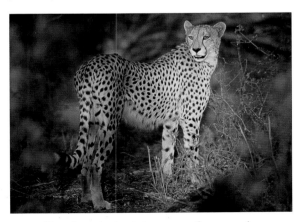

ABOVE Cheetah are daytime hunters, most often seen early morning and late afternoon on open woodlands.

Poetry in motion. The cheetah is the fastest and arguably the most beautiful of land mammals, able to reach 70 kilometres per hour within three seconds from a standing start and 100 kilometres per hour at full throttle. With its streamlined body, long and powerful legs, deep chest, supple spine – and a long tail to give it balance – it is superbly built for speed. But physical specialisation has its price. The animal lacks stamina: during the explosive chase its temperature rises and it cannot sustain the effort for more than a few seconds. And when it does manage a kill, it is exhausted and has to rest – an invitation to the hyaenas and vultures to move in.

The cheetah is a highly endangered species, especially vulnerable to habitat loss (much of the open plains country, its natural environment, has been taken over by ranchers and farmers) and from competition from bigger and stronger predators. Cheetahs generally hunt during the cooler times of the day by stalking their prey and then making a quick dash for the kill. Female cheetahs are independent creatures, living for the most part in solitary splendour, their only company their latest litter of four to six cubs. The male is needed only for breeding purposes.

Experienced game rangers are sometimes able to reach
close proximity to cheetahs that have become used to
human company. Many animals tend to ignore a vehicle,
but dare to step out of the vehicle and the situation will
change immediately – to fight or flight. Cheetahs are
accomplished hunters, though much has been sacrificed
in the interests of speed. The animal cannot, for instance,
rotate the wrists of its forelimbs, an adaptation that helps
keep it steady during the lightning-fast pursuit but also
inhibits its agility when the prey – a lively impala perhaps –
changes direction at the last moment.

In a pride of lions, it is the female who does the hard work, and never more so than during the hunt. This is a highly cooperative affair, full of subtlety and skill. Usually, one of the lionesses will lie hidden in ambush while the others stampede the herd in order to isolate the weakest, and then drive it towards their waiting sister (or mother). It is only when the chase is over that the regal males move in to claim the choicest parts of the kill. A group effort will often account for more than one prey victim (a remarkable seven wildebeest kills have been recorded in a single attack). Working as a group also enables the pride to protect its meal against the inevitable scavengers, which arrive on the scene long before the carcass turns cold. Hyaenas are formidable competitors for the dead meat; jackals are cheekily accomplished thieves; vultures have numbers and determination on their side.

A pride of lion usually comprises related females and their cubs plus one or more adult males (sometimes a single male holds tenure). The males do not compete for female favours: it's an equal-opportunity society. And these animals show remarkable stamina in the mating process: during the female's five-day oestrus period she will couple once every 20 minutes or so. Often, all the pride's females will come into oestrus at the same time, which is nature's way of maintaining the stability of the pride – if only one female were available, suitors would fight each other, with hugely destructive results. Up to four cubs are born, which their mother hides away for a few weeks before bringing them into the pride's crèche.

Close encounter. The best times to see lions in the bushveld are in the early morning and late afternoon: they tend to lie up in dense vegetation during the hotter hours. In the coolness of winter, though, they are a lot more diurnal and visible. Most of their hunting forays take place near a river or water hole, especially in times of drought.

Featured in these and the previous pages is the most secretive of the bushveld's larger carnivores, and encounters like the one shown above are rare. Indeed, leopards can live in an area for years without being detected, even by a skilled ranger. The cat, well camouflaged by its dappled coat, is cautious and silent by habit, solitary, lurking unnoticed among the tumbled rocks of a koppie (hillock) or in a dense patch of bushveld. It will also take to the branches of a tree. Very occasionally it may emerge onto open ground. Leopards are highly adaptable creatures with a catholic diet – they will eat anything that moves, from a small rat right up to a full-grown wildebeest, from an insect to a fish (some individuals are expert swimmers) – and sometimes things that don't move, too, like the carcass of another predator's kill. Given a choice, though, they will favour a small to medium-sized antelope or, very occasionally, a baboon. In the latter case, however, it attacks by night, quickly snatching its sleeping victim and beating a hasty retreat. To confront a troop of these sharp-fanged primates by daylight is to court humiliation, perhaps even death.

This is a highly unusual sighting of a mating pair of of leopards in a tree, in this case a jackalberry, one of their favourite retreats. The leopard is quite at home in trees, often hauling its kill onto the higher branches – a remarkable feat of physical strength because the prey can weigh a lot more than its predator. This stratagem keeps the cat's meal safe from marauding hyaenas and from the ever-present vultures wheeling in the sky above. The sharp-eyed birds cannot see through the canopy and, in any event, do not perch in order to eat. Essentially, though, leopards are not an arboreal species, taking to the trees only to protect their kill, to escape bigger predators (notably lion) and, sometimes, simply to relax. Cubs are hidden away among the rocks, in a thicket or in an old antbear burrow until they are about nine months old, when they begin to hunt for themselves, starting with small prey such as an infant scrub hare or an impala lamb.

When it comes to opportunism, the spotted hyaena is king of the veld, willing to take more or less anything that presents itself and doing so both cleverly and, often, bravely. A pack has been known to tree a full-grown lion in order to commandeer the carcass of its prey (though they often come off second best in such encounters). Hyaenas have well-developed senses of smell and hearing, and sight: they invariably keep an eye on airborne vultures, following the movements of these big, bold birds in order to locate a meal. But they are also fine hunters as well as enterprising scavengers, moving in groups, cooperating closely to isolate one of the weaker animals in a herd. They are not especially quick on their feet but have enormous stamina, and the strength of their jaws is legendary.

ABOVE AND TOP RIGHT Young wild dogs in their den area. In a typical pack, only the dominant female and male – known as the alpha pair – are permitted to breed. The other members remain chaste, devoting their energies to helping feed and rear the pups and guarding the den. Or so it was thought until fairly recently. It now appears, though, that a second pair will sometimes mate, and that the alpha female, depending on her mood, may accept her rival's offspring and even help raise them. On the other hand, she might well, if food is scarce for example, kill the pups.

OPPOSITE Wild dogs are among Africa's most endangered mammals even though the species, in theory anyway, has so much going for it – fearlessness, resourcefulness, intelligence, the ability to cooperate, and hunting prowess. They have been known to tree a leopard and chase hyaenas from a kill. Their small numbers, of course, have a lot to do with the way they have been treated by farmers who consider them a danger to their stock. Their ranges have been drastically reduced. Moreover, they have a surprisingly short lifespan (about six years), which may be the result of inbreeding and the consequent deterioration of the gene pool.

The Hunted

The most visible of the Lowveld's animals are the impalas, medium-sized antelope that look and behave a little like springbok but have their own, very distinctive character. There are so many of these herbivores – more than 100 000 of them in Kruger alone – that one hardly notices them after the first few hours of a game-viewing trip. For visitors, they soon become just part of the scenery. For carnivores, they serve as the ordinary meal of the day.

But impala are really worth much more than a passing glance. They are graceful creatures, and remarkable ones as well, delicate, bright, alert and, as a herd, sheer poetry in motion. Startle a group and they will bound away across the veld in a succession of breathtaking leaps, often rising effortlessly three metres and more in the air, moving in unison, covering the ground in an almost ballet-like choreography of sweeping ascents, descents and fluid changes of direction. Only the males bear horns, which are elegantly lyre-like and deeply ringed. The males, too, compete

ABOVE The roan antelope is easily identified by its mask markings and large ears. Both males and females carry horns.

ABOVE Impala are the most populous of South Africa's ungulates (hoofed animals). In flight from a predator, the impala often performs acrobatic leaps in order to evade its pursuer. Many carnivores include impala in their diet, so these antelope are always on alert.

aggressively for territory and for their own harems, and are noisy in the process, sometimes with disconcerting effect: the cacophony of barks, snorts, growls and roars they make can be (and sometimes is) mistaken for the sounds of lion.

Also a favoured prey of the big cats is the blue wildebeest, another gregarious bovid which is related to the antelope. This is a heavy, horned animal with a thick neck and spindly legs, and it gathers in numbers on the east-central and southern grasslands. Oddly enough, the herds often mingle with plains (or Burchell's) zebra, an association that rewards both parties – the zebras find security in numbers, and the wildebeest benefit from their guests' acute senses and ability to give early warning of danger.

At first glance it seems that one zebra looks very much the same as another, but in fact no two individuals have the identical stripe pattern, giving each one its own 'fingerprint'. More puzzling, perhaps, is why evolution thought it necessary to give the zebra stripes at all: the neat markings

stand out like a beacon against the flat colours of the savanna. But evolution seldom makes mistakes, and never when it comes to hardy survivors like these. The stripes may dazzle but they also confuse lions and other carnivores, blurring the zebra's outline, especially when the animals are grouped together. Predators don't have colour vision and are hard put to single out one individual from the psychedelic jumble of a herd. Just how effective the camouflage is becomes clear when one remembers that navies began painting their warships with stripes during the Second World War.

Handsomest of the herbivores is, without doubt, the sable antelope, a large, regal animal with great curving horns, high at the shoulder and clothed in a shiny black coat (a glossy brown in the female) with pure white patches on the face, belly and rump. Sables live in herds of about 30 and occur throughout the region, but are usually best seen along the road from Kruger's Phalaborwa Gate east to the Letaba rest camp.

A lot more difficult to spot is the eland, largest of the region's antelope and not nearly as attractive as the sable. It looks like something designed by a committee: pot-bellied, dewlapped, hunchbacked, with a disproportionately small head. The 650-kilogram animal usually lives in small groups of six or so (occasionally in herds of up to a hundred), treasures its privacy and keeps well away from tourist roads.

Also large and rather ungainly looking is the tsessebe, an otherwise unremarkable antelope with one surprising claim to distinction – it is the swiftest of all bovids. And it has stamina to match: it can run faster and sustain its speed for a longer time than a horse; adults reach speeds of 60 kilometres an hour and more. Tsessebe are most commonly seen in the mopane scrublands north of the Letaba River.

Much more sedate and arguably better looking is the nyala, a medium-sized animal sporting beautiful lyre horns and an unusually shaggy, purplish coat marked by vertical stripes. Lions, leopards and wild dogs find the nyala a particularly tasty prey, but it usually gives as good as it gets: its horns are formidable weapons.

ABOVE Zebra are especially numerous along Kruger's eastern boundary and in the central grasslands.

Larger and rather more elegant is the kudu, which has a slender build, a massive neck and, like the nyala but even more striking, a magnificent pair of horns, neatly spiralled and growing to an impressive 1.5 metres in length. Males reach a mass of about 250 kilograms; females are smaller (160 kilograms) and hornless. When kudu are disturbed they will thunder away through the bush, easily negotiating the thickets, the bulls raising their chins so that their horns are tilted back almost horizontally. The species is found mainly in the well-wooded and hilly parts of the Lowveld, though it does have a fairly wide habitat tolerance. None of the major predators really fancy tangling with a full-grown male kudu.

Lions do target roan antelope, however, but here too they rarely risk a one-on-one confrontation. The roan is among the rarer of the herbivores, partly, because of the high rate of infant mortality. The female gives birth to a single calf at any time of the year but most often in the summer months, and then hides it in the bush for a few weeks. It is at this time that the species is at its most vulnerable, easy prey for hyaena and jackal, cheetah, caracal and other carnivores with a good sense of smell. Older calves are inclined to freeze when threatened, which pretty well invites death.

Among the several other kinds of Lowveld antelope are two hill-loving species. The mountain reedbuck, once widespread through southern Africa, is now confined to just a few game farms and sanctuaries (including the Eastern Cape's Mountain Zebra National Park). In Kruger, it hides away in the foothills of the Lebombo range and in the rugged area near Malelane in the south. The klipspringer, on the other hand, prefers the outcrops of Kruger's far eastern and, especially, far northern parts. This little creature is a master of the rock scramble, displaying dainty agility and a superb sense of balance, and is often seen standing on tiptoe on a boulder with its hooves bunched together. When pushed, it somehow manages to run up rock faces seemingly climbable only by baboons and the more skilled of mountaineers.

ABOVE The kudu is a large antelope easily recognised by its long, spiral-shaped horns. They are never far from a water source.

The Lowveld is sanctuary to well over 30 000 Burchell's (or plains) zebra, a species that favours the savanna parklands and grasslands. The species is often seen in large aggregations, but within these are numerous smaller one-stallion breeding units and bachelor groups. Often, too, the animals mix in with the wildebeest and antelope herds, a mutually rewarding association: they find safety in numbers, and their hosts benefit from the zebras' keen senses of sight, smell and hearing. Numbers, however, are not the zebra's only means of defence: it can both bite and kick, sometimes lethally, when attacked by smaller predators such as hyaenas, cheetahs and wild dogs.

Like the zebra, blue wildebeest are creatures of the grassy plains of the central and southern Lowveld, sometimes congregating in herds of a hundred and more. The animal, also known as the gnu, was once widespread across the northern parts of the country but has suffered grievously from the depredations of stock farmers and, inevitably, from hunting. Fences in particular have proved devastating, serving as barriers to a species that migrates en masse to its historic drinking sites in times of drought. The Kruger National Park hosts more than 10 000 head, found most abundantly to the southeast of the Letaba River. Pictured at right are two territorial bulls.

The magical sunset hour. Rangers exchange ideas (above) while a greater kudu (right) begins to settle down for the night. Kudu are browsers, favouring areas covered by small trees. Only the males have horns, which are spiralled and magnificent, and they are bigger than the females – which, oddly enough, may account for a general imbalance among the herds. Males tend to be outnumbered by the females, a consequence of their need for more food (a liability in lean times), and are perhaps less agile in avoiding lions and spotted hyaenas, their principal predators.

Like the kudu, the male waterbuck is renowned for its splendid horns, which are long, heavily ringed and forward-curving affairs that serve as the animal's tertiary but often highly effective line of defence (first and second choices are seclusion and flight respectively). The lion is the animal's main enemy, but it also falls victim to hyaenas, leopards, cheetahs and, because waterbuck seldom stray far from water, to crocodiles.

The omnipresent impala, a delicate and fleet-footed medium-sized antelope, graces the savanna woodlands of the Lowveld's central and southern parts in its tens of thousands. Predictably, these animals rank among the favoured species of the larger carnivores, so they are quick to sense danger. Having done so, the male gives a rasping, incongruously loud and deep-throated call and the whole herd then bounds away to safety. The leaps are both prodigious and elegant, and are often performed even when there is no obstacle in the way.

LEFT The dainty little klipspringer ('rock-jumper') is perfectly at home in the boulder-strewn granite hills that dot the Lowveld landscape. The antelope are not often seen by visitors, living as they do among the remoter koppies, isolated from the mass of other herbivores that inhabit the open plains.

BELOW Also small, shy and attractive is the tiny steenbok ('stone buck'). Again, this slender antelope is not easily spotted – its colours blend perfectly into the dun-and-yellow surrounds. The animals are at their most visible when they nibble, usually in pairs, at the short roadside grasses.

OPPOSITE The most physically impressive of the Lowveld's antelope is undoubtedly the sable, of which there are about 2 000 individuals. Prime elements of its majestic appearance are its horns, of course, its height at the shoulder, its mane and its glossy chestnut coat.

Giants of the Veld

The big guys of the bushveld are the champions of their own environments – hippos and crocodiles along the rivers; giraffe in the woodlands; white rhino and buffalo in the grasslands; black rhino where the browsing is good; and elephant just about everywhere.

The rhinos are something of a throwback, relics of those ancient of days when the megaherbivores ruled the earth. These are massive creatures, the males weighing anything up to two tonnes, lethally horned (the record length is an impressive 1.58 metres), with hides like armour plate, and they are surprisingly nimble for such bulky beasts. They have no natural enemies, except man – but, in Africa, that is enemy enough. Rhino horn is a much-prized commodity in the Far East as a fever suppressant and in the Middle East as an aphrodisiac and for its ornamental uses. The result is that the animal has been hunted to near extinction.

Today, of the tens of thousands that once roamed the continent, just 4 000 or so rhino remain. In the Lowveld they disappeared entirely, and occur there now only by courtesy of Ian Player (brother of golfer Gary) and his colleagues at the Natal Parks Board who, almost half a century ago, developed innovative drug-darting techniques in order to capture and translocate the animals. Small breeding herds were then established in distant places, to be nurtured until their survival and growth was assured. The Kruger National Park's pioneer white rhinos arrived there in the early 1960s, and they thrived. Some 10 years later 20 of their black cousins joined them.

ABOVE *A hippo's yawn could mean either aggression or, when there is a female nearby, what humans might term 'affection'.*

Not that the two forms come into much, if any, contact with each other in the field. They are different species, each with its own needs and favoured environment: the white variety is in fact dark grey in colour (the adjective comes from the Afrikaans word for 'wide', a reference to the square-lipped mouth of the grazing mammal). By contrast, the black rhino (again, a misleading term) is a browser, its pointed mouth perfectly designed for its diet of leaves and branches. It is also the smaller and more aggressive of the two, quite prepared to charge if an intruder appears on its patch (though this bravado is usually a bluff). It doesn't see too well, but has excellent senses of smell and hearing.

Comparable in size is the hippopotamus, a semi-aquatic 1 500-kilogram behemoth with a huge yawn and tusk-like teeth that can (and in parts of Africa still does) chew a small river-craft to pieces. The yawn can mean one of two or more things, depending on the company the animal is keeping. If it's with a female, the gesture indicates something approaching what we would term 'affection'. If there are other bulls around, though, it means 'back off', and this can be the prelude to a territorial fight of quite titanic proportions.

Water, of course, is the hippo's milieu, and indeed it cannot remain on dry land for long in the daytime because

ABOVE *Giraffe have a fairly loose social structure – individuals will associate with a number of herds during their lives. Males are more solitary. From a distance, gender can often be identified by observing that males reach up to eat and females tend to eat at head height or below.*

ABOVE Game-viewing in the private Sabi Sabi reserve ranks high among the better-known and most rewarding safari destinations.

its skin, thick as it may be, is highly sensitive to the hot sun. Unsurprisingly, therefore, it prefers to graze at night, foraging near river or pan when it can, but able in lean times to travel up to 30 kilometres at night in search of new pastures.

Sharing the hippo's environment is the Nile crocodile, a giant, primeval reptile that ranks as the closest surviving relative of the dinosaurs. This ancient and formidable life form can grow to a length of six metres, live for 100 years, and is

ABOVE In much of Africa, the elephant has suffered from poachers' predations, but on the southern subcontinent it flourishes.

superbly designed for hunting by ambush: the positioning of its ears, nostrils and eyes is such that it can lie in wait, almost completely submerged and barely noticeable to the unsuspecting animals and birds (and people) who pass by. At other times it impersonates a log floating in the water and then, with explosive suddenness, seizes its hapless victim – an impala perhaps, or a waterfowl – in its vice-like jaws and drags it down into the depths to drown.

The story that crocs eat their young is pure myth: they are in fact excellent parents. The female lays her eggs in the sandy soil of a riverbank and keeps close watch for the 12-week incubation. When she hears the hatchlings squeaking inside their shells she helps them out and, with infinite care, carries them in her mouth to the water. Here they remain for several months, during which time there is constant communication between adults and offspring, and between the youngsters themselves. As each new batch arrives, their elder siblings welcome them with soft greetings, and thereafter they keep calling reassuringly to each other.

Tallest of mammals is the giraffe, one of evolution's special wonders. It also ranks among the four heaviest of land animals, reaching a weight of anything up to 1.5 tonnes. Its freakishly long neck, developed over millennia to enable it to feed off the shoots and young leaves atop the trees, places an enormous distance between heart and brain – too far, one would think, for the heart to pump life-sustaining blood all the way up. But nature has devised a cunning system of arteries, and valves in the larger veins. Without these mechanical refinements the animal's brain would starve when it stands upright, and become flooded when it bends down to drink.

For all its size, though, the giraffe is vulnerable to predators, notably to lions and especially when it slakes its thirst at riverside or water hole. At these times, with its legs splayed, it is more or less immobilised. Away from water, though, it becomes a different customer altogether: it can cover the ground at speed and, if cornered, delivers a lethal kick.

The African buffalo and the elephant both number among the Lowveld's charismatic Big Five (the others are lion, leopard and rhino). Buffalo are everywhere to be seen, sometimes in herds of up to 200 individuals. The species is distinguished by its bulk (800 kilograms) and by the bony boss atop its head from which great horns curve up. Treat the buffalo with respect; keep well away from those solitary bulls, which often lurk around water holes.

Not quite so numerous but also readily visible are the elephants – usually gentle creatures that can often be watched from vehicles stationed within very close proximity to them. In large parts of Africa, the animals have been poached (for the ivory of their tusks) to regional extinction, but on the southern subcontinent good management has allowed the herds to grow and flourish – rather too well in the Lowveld. They can do enormous damage to the environment (an adult's daily intake runs at about 300 kilograms, and it will topple an entire tree just to get at the few fresh leaves at the top). Various methods have been tried in the drive to control elephant numbers including, controversially, culling the great herds. This remains an ongoing issue of debate.

ABOVE Rhinos can produce a surprising turn of speed, but the rare display of anger usually turns out to be bravado.

Elephants are the largest of the terrestrial mammals, an adult weighing up to six tonnes and reaching a shoulder height of about 3.5 metres (one Namibian leviathan was recorded to have been 4.42 metres high). Tusk length varies from region to region, depending on the gene pool and the environment; those of the Addo Elephant National Park in the Eastern Cape, for instance, tend to be small. One Kruger bull, the renowned Mufanyane ('The Irritable One') bore two perfectly matched tusks each weighing 55 kilograms; those of a Kenyan specimen, shot in 1897, had a combined weight of nearly 200 kilograms.

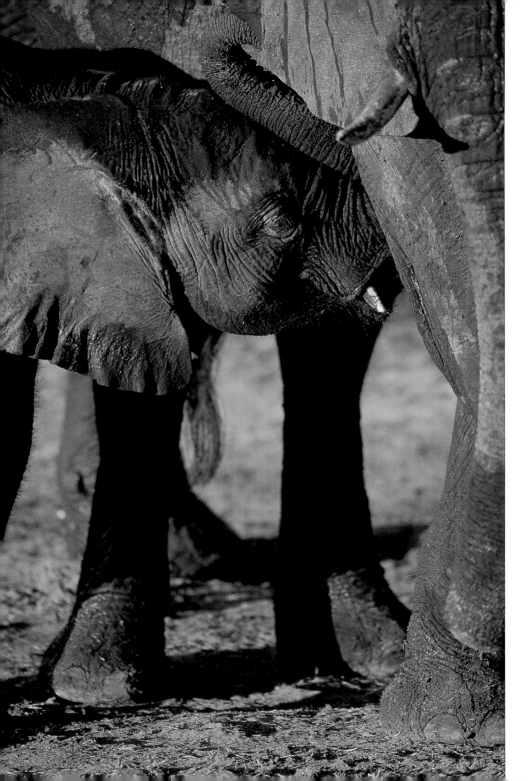

Ranked among the bushveld's Big Five, elephants are gregarious giants, usually seen in small herds of females and their offspring. They are led by an unchallenged matriarch, and are joined by bulls only for mating purposes. For the rest, adult males spend their days in bachelor groups or, rarely, roam the great spaces in solitary splendour. The family groups often mix with others to browse a loosely defended clan territory. These great creatures seem to be peculiarly sensitive to injury or a death among their number – a remarkable characteristic in the non-primate world. If one dies, for example, the others will trumpet their distress and stand guard over the corpse.

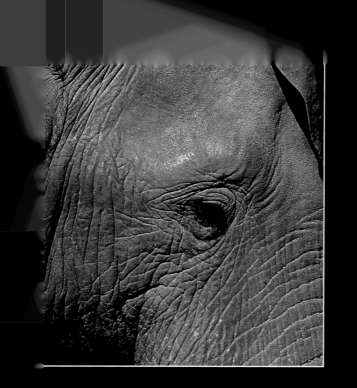

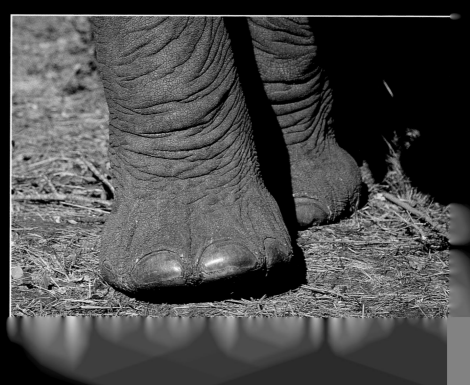

PREVIOUS PAGES Water is a magnet for elephants, serving variously as bath, playground and cooling agent. This last is an important element: heat and a large body do not sit well together, and a good wallow in mud, with the occasional trunk-squirted shower, helps make the midday hours much more bearable.

OPPOSITE From left to right and top to bottom: elephant eye; thick, deeply scored hide; fly-whisk tail; feet, and more feet which, surprisingly enough, the animal uses to scrape bulbs and tasty grasses from the earth.

TOP LEFT AND TOP RIGHT The trunk and tusks are the elephant's main food-gathering tools. The former is, considering its size, remarkably sensitive, and able to pick up individual fruits and pluck single grass stems. The tusks are used for defence, of course, but also to strip bark from trees and dig up roots.

RIGHT The elephant's large ears act as a unique cooling system. The veins on the back carry blood close to the surface of the skins so that when the elephant flaps its ears, the movement of air helps lower the temperature of the blood in the veins.

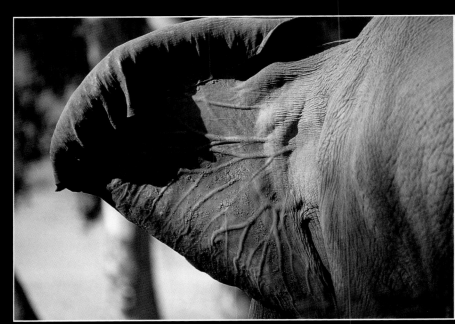

THESE PAGES Placid though the buffalo seems, it is in fact ranked among the most fearless, and most dangerous, of African mammals. Lions are its only natural enemy, and even the big cats tend to choose discretion before valour. In a one-on-one confrontation, the lion may well come second, and if the buffalo does lose, it goes down fighting to its last breath. Remarkably, the herd will actually come to the aid of one of its own under attack from a pride and drive away the carnivores. Usually, though, they try to make it as difficult as possible for the lions to select a victim, forming an outward-facing protective circle with the bulls at the front.

OVERLEAF, LEFT AND RIGHT African buffalo, like elephants, are good swimmers, feel at home in the water, and like nothing better than a good wallow in a muddy pool. They are a common sight in the Lowveld region, with aggregations of up to a thousand having been observed in the area. They are also inquisitive animals, often raising their great heads to stare at your vehicle. They may take a few steps towards you, snorting and sweeping their heads and horns from side to side, but this signifies nothing except curiosity: buffalo are usually harmless unless they are directly threatened.

The Lowveld sanctuaries, and most notably the Kruger National Park, have helped pioneer the rescue of the rhino, once one of Africa's most endangered mammals. Both species, white and black, were locally extinct until just a few decades ago, and their numbers were severely depleted elsewhere. But the southern animals survived; a few were relocated from the Natal parks, and the future of the rhino is now, hopefully, secure.

White rhinos can most often be seen in the well-watered grasslands situated between the Crocodile and Sabie rivers, usually visiting their watering places as the sun sets or soon after nightfall. The species is generally even-tempered, but there is nevertheless a distinct hierarchy within the group itself, and white rhino bulls will fight fiercely for dominance and the favours of the females.

Some privately run bushveld sanctuaries lay on horseback excursions, which are safe enough providing there aren't any big carnivores around. Here (above), giraffe view visitors with equanimity. These tall blondes are among Africa's most gentle creatures – and, in evolutionary terms, among the most remarkable. Apart from the ingenious system of valves, which ensures that enough blood reaches the brain (see page 53), nature has devised an unusually large heart – nearly three per cent of the body mass – and an extraordinarily tough one, too, with walls a good seven centimetres thick. Giraffe are found in groups of anything between four and 50; bulls are known for their 'necking' behaviour, a ritualistic fight to establish dominance.

LEFT AND OPPOSITE Hippos – great semi-aquatic mammals – are surprisingly good swimmers despite their size, and are well able to submerge themselves for five minutes or even longer without taking in air. In the deeper water, they actually walk along the riverbed.

RIGHT There are few substantial stretches of Lowveld water that do not host their resident hippos. This is their milieu, and indeed they cannot stay on land for any great length of time – at least during the daylight hours. Their thick skins are highly sensitive to the hot sun. At night, though, they come ashore to forage near river or dam and sometimes, when the grazing is poor, they will travel up to 30 kilometres in search of better pasture.

The hippopotamus and the crocodile are the Big Two of the inland waters, the latter most often seen basking in the warmth of the sun on mudbanks or boulders, often in company with others of its kind. The crocodile does this in order to gain heat, like all reptiles must. The crocodile's favoured prey are generally medium-sized antelope, but especially large and aggressive specimens have been known to take full-grown lions, buffaloes and even giraffe. Crocodiles are said to be the most 'intelligent' of the reptiles even though their brains are little bigger than a man's thumb. They are quick to adapt to new environments and develop new skills.

The Other Players

To human eyes, the warthog is arguably the least prepossessing of bushveld animals: it has a long snout, small upward-curving tusks, 'warts' on its face and a disproportionately large head. But in many ways it's quite an admirable creature, tough, courageous, well adapted to the savanna and woodland country in which it lives. You will invariably spot it in nuclear family groups, father (the boar), mother (sow) and offspring (piglets) trotting through the bush, their tails pointing skywards. The hard snout serves as a scoop for digging up roots and tubers, and for clearing earth from the burrow. In fact the whole head is used as a food-gathering tool and a battering ram – against leopard (its chief predator), lion, cheetah and, less often, wild dog. The tusks are a deadly defensive addition; the warty protruberances protect the eyes.

The warthog is one of a panoply of smaller animals that may not immediately impress but that nevertheless have their fascinations and which, together, comprise the bulk of the Lowveld's mammals. Remarkable in both their number and variety, these include the baboons and vervet monkeys among the primates; bat-eared foxes; numerous members of the cat family, such as the civet, the beautiful serval and the caracal (a handsome hunter that is related to the northern hemisphere's lynxes); the polecat, mongooses, genets, wide-eyed bushbabies (now more officially known as galagos); the aardvark and aardwolf; the honey badger (also known as the ratel) which, pound for pound, is perhaps the toughest of the bushveld creatures; pangolins, porcupines, dassies (hyraxes), bats and rats. And more.

ABOVE The vervet is one of two monkey species of the region. They are excellent climbers and at night seek refuge in large trees.

Among the more watchable of the array are the chacma baboons, intriguing for, among other things, their often all-too-human behaviour, responses and relationships. If you look long enough at a troop, you'll see displays of pretty well all human emotions, virtues and vices – courage, cowardice and deceitfulness, greed, envy and generosity, strength and natural leadership. Each member has his or her own, quite distinct, personality, but one quality, an intense sociability, is common to all and this, together with a varied diet, intelligence, opportunism and the ability to adapt, makes the baboon a supreme survivor and a fascinating subject of study.

The baboon spends the daytime hours in groups – which may be 40 or even 50 strong but occasionally number 100 or so – foraging for fruits, roots, bulbs, grubs, insects, scorpions and other small food items. When chance offers up a larger and more meaty meal – a bird, perhaps, a hare, even a small antelope – it will gratefully accept the bonus. The troop is led by a big, bold and bossy male, a dictator who decides where and when to move, when to flee and when to fight. The troop covers the ground in a kind of 'battle order', with the females and youngsters in the middle, the tougher and more senior males to either side, the lower ranks at front and rear. Rank in fact is everything to this animal, the hierarchy

ABOVE Ever alert, tree squirrels constantly watch out for danger. This usually comes in the form of a predatory bird or a host of ground-dwelling carnivores. If a predator is seen while in a safe location, it will tease the attacker by shaking its tail and making sharp alarm calls.

unashamedly chauvinist: all adult males are dominant over all females. But within that broad arrangement there's an intricate and ever-changing network of personal friendships and alliances, bonds that are cemented through the agency of grooming.

One common misconception is that baboons post 'sentries' when they are out and about or, come dusk, when they settle down to sleep. The belief probably derives from the primate's inquisitive nature: a baboon will often climb up to a vantage point simply to see what's happening in the countryside around.

Of special note among the smaller carnivores is the caracal, a strikingly beautiful, lithe, pointy-eared 20-kilogram cat that is renowned for its fierce nature and quite remarkable agility. This is a widely distributed species in southern Africa (it is also found in the Middle East) but rarely seen, happily perhaps because it is more than willing to take the offensive if it feels threatened. So quick are its reflexes that it is able, from a standing position, to catch a bird on the wing, its powerful hind legs propelling it anything up to five metres high to pluck its startled quarry from the air.

ABOVE During the day a troop of chacma baboons, perhaps 50 strong, has made its way across the veld in search of fruits, bulbs and edible roots. These primates, though, are not wholly vegetarian: they will take scorpions and the larger insects and even birds and young antelope.

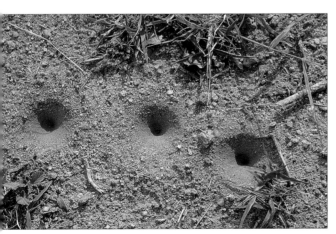

ABOVE During the larval stage, antlions dig a conical trap in the sand in order to catch passing ants in their pincer-like jaws.

It was long thought that the caracal's diet comprised largely rodents and dassies, but recent studies reveal it is quite capable of taking largish antelope – impala, for example – that are more than twice its size. It catches its food by a combination of silent stalking and lightning-quick pounces, and it will guard the carcass with unbridled vigour, spitting and hissing at the jackals and other scavengers that hover at mealtimes.

Fearless, too, is the honey badger, a compact little (12-kilogram) bundle of energy, courage, aggression and pure muscle, which will face down just about any threat with bared teeth and snarling defiance. Paradoxically, though, it remains a generally shy animal (almost all life forms prefer discretion to valour), usually retreating to its burrow when disturbed or – its second line of defence – emitting a smell that is just as noxious, if not more so, than that of a skunk, and certainly off-putting enough to repel most predators.

These badgers are omnivores, feeding on fruits, bulbs, lizards, snakes, rodents, grubs and spiders. They have also been known to bring down a small antelope. The creature's fondness for honey is legendary: it seeks out bee hives and

destroys them with its razor-sharp teeth and strong claws. In this it is often helped by the tiny greater honeyguide, a bird that shows the way to the hive with excited displays, waits for the carnage to be completed, and then joins in the feast.

The honey badger has also been known to dispatch a full-grown rock python, Africa's largest snake. This is not, though, the most dangerous of the reptiles, killing its prey by slow constriction – a surprisingly rare event (captive specimens have been known to go for anything up to two years without food). Species that merit a far wider berth are the black mamba, which grows up to four metres, is quite aggressive, and common, often lying up in abandoned burrows and termite nests. Its venom is neurotoxic (that is, it attacks the nervous system) and fast-acting. Much less adventurous and somewhat smaller are the Egyptian (or banded) and the spitting cobras. The latter actually does spit its poison – at the eyes, very accurately, and from several metres. Most often seen is the African puff adder, which is also highly venomous but a sluggish creature that depends on camouflage to avoid detection. It moves only when stumbled on. Watch your step.

THESE PAGES Profile of a warthog. The pig-like animal has a disproportionately large head and short legs, and must kneel when feeding. Distinctive, too, is the way it enters its burrow – backwards. This makes sense, because in doing so it covers its back and any pursuing predator will have to face a formidable pair of tusks.

LEFT AND ABOVE One of only two of the larger primates occuring in the Lowveld (the other is the baboon), the lively vervet monkey spends most of its days foraging in wooded areas. Its diet comprises insects, leaves and ripe fruits, which the animal unerringly selects because it has sharp colour vision. One of its more remarkable features is the sound, or rather the series of sounds, it makes. A prime target of carnivores, each different alarm call signifies a particular predator – a sharp bark warns of an approaching snake, while a chutter tells of an eagle in the vicinity.

OPPOSITE, LEFT AND RIGHT The dog-faced chacma baboon is a common Lowveld resident: it is estimated that there are somewhat more than 120 separate troops in the Kruger National Park alone, with a combined population of around 40 000. A strict ranking system is maintained within each troop: there can be several dominant males but only one supreme leader, usually a big animal with personality and the ability to bluff – which is how he keeps his position, although occasional fights do erupt.

LEFT Most common of the mongooses is the dwarf species, often seen perched on a termite mound. This is a pack animal with a well-developed system of cooperative detection of and defence against predators and, especially, against birds of prey. Colonies average nine members. Most of the offspring are produced by the dominant pair, and the younger mongooses help with the rearing, grooming, feeding, carrying and, often, the babysitting of the litter.

ABOVE The endearing greater galago is more commonly known as the thick-tailed bushbaby, a name derived from the animal's childlike cries. This is one of the larger and most sociable of these nocturnal primates, though it is capable of leaping prodigiously from one tree to another.

BELOW Even though savagely persecuted as a pest, the handsome little black-backed jackal remains one of the most common of South Africa's carnivores, present in numbers in those rural areas from which the large predators have disappeared but also, surprisingly, close to urban centres too. It is a highly adaptable species, able to adjust to and flourish in a wide variety of environments. Its main defence is masterly concealment: it has the ability to keep the lowest of profiles.

RIGHT The pretty little tree squirrel likes to bask in the sun, but for the most part remains hard to detect. Often the first indication of its presence is an alarm call – a chuckling sound when there's a snake around, and a whistle when a bird of prey appears.

Below A stately grey heron in the shallows of the Sabie River. The bird is distinguished by its white head and neck, as well as the chracteristic black eye strip that forms a feathery plume at the nape of its neck.

Opposite The odd-looking secretary bird most often comes into view striding along the ground with measured tread, but it does fly well and roosts in trees. The species' common name probably derives not from its black crest-feathers (which resemble the quill pens of a mediaeval secretary) but from the Arabic *saqr-et-tair*, meaning 'hunter-bird'.

LEFT Invariably heard giving its piercing three- or four-note call from the top of a Lowveld tree is the scarlet-chested sunbird, an attractive species that feeds on insects, spiders and, mostly, on nectar.

BELOW As its name suggests, the whitefronted bee-eater lives on a diet of flying insects, which it takes on the wing. Its favourite meal is a butterfly.

OPPOSITE Dressed entirely in grey and with a large crest, the grey lourie is also known as the 'go-away bird' due to his distinctive call, which sounds poetically like 'go-away'.

ABOVE A huge bird with a huge beak, the saddlebilled stork is invariably seen standing motionless in the still water of the shallows, occasionally walking in stately manner, looking for fish, stirring the mud to see what delicacies emerge.

ABOVE Insects comprise the lilacbreasted roller's diet. The bird is a resident of the denser woodland areas, more commonly perhaps in the northern parts of the Lowveld. It usually occurs in pairs or small groups of three or four.

ABOVE The chicken-sized helmeted guineafowl lives in the open grassland and savanna areas in flocks that can number in the hundreds. The bird eats both plant matter and insects, sometimes picking ticks from the hide of a warthog.

ABOVE The yellowbilled hornbill is a medium-sized bird that forages mostly at ground level for the fruits and seeds that make up most of its food intake. This is a common bushveld, savanna and woodland species.

The Fabric of Life

The Lowveld is a botanist's delight: a vast diversity of flora – trees and shrubs, flowering plants, bulbs, worts, grasses – finds sanctuary in a region with more than its share of different vegetation zones. The soil here is generally fertile, the climate generous enough.

For the lover of trees, there are more than 400 species to study and enjoy, many with evocative names – the velvet bushwillow, ironwood, yellowwood and Natal mahogany, mountain syringae, sumach bean, sausage tree, tamboti, bride's bush, raintree, the familiar marula and thorny acacia. Near the rivers you will find giant, twisty-rooted sycamore figs and, in the north, the pale-barked, ghostly fever tree. Among the most beautiful species is the nyala tree, a majestic evergreen with a dense, rounded crown.

ABOVE A commonly found climber, the wild morning glory has a flower up to 60 millimetres in diameter. Flowering from February to April, these colourful blooms range from a light pink to a deep purple.

ABOVE Delicate impala, the most numerous of the larger mammals, feed on the short grasses of the south and central areas.

Most visitors come to the region mainly for its animals, of course, not for its flora. Nor for its insects, of which there are countless numbers and uncounted species. Like the array of trees on display, though, insect life is rich, fascinating, and a highly significant element of the ecosystem. Collectively, the insects, arachnids and other arthropods make up fully half of all the earth's living organisms (including plants) and a large percentage of the total biomass. Some types are disease bearing, dangerous to man and beast, but the majority are harmless, indeed beneficial, serving as efficient pollinators and as essential conduits for the cyclical flow of nutrients.

All these forms of life – vertebrates, invertebrates, plants, plus immeasurable numbers of micro-organisms that lie beneath the visible fabric – combine to create a coherent environment, a system of gene pools in infinitely delicate balance, and in which the fragile cycle of life is sustained by collective dependence.

Nothing is wasted in the bushveld (nor in any wilderness for that matter). When an animal is killed or dies of old age, starvation or sickness, the large scavengers move in, to be followed by smaller ones and by the flies and maggots, by bacteria and by invisible creatures that subsist on bone tissue, and finally there is no sustenance left in the carcass: it all, eventually, returns to the soil to enrich it and to sustain other types and new generations of living things. No dying tree remains untouched, no dead branch, no fallen leaf. No waste.

Among the best known of nature's vacuum cleaners are the tiny dung beetles that have an extraordinary ability to locate and remove the droppings of mammals, sometimes converging with astonishing speed and in vast numbers (around 7 000 individuals have been observed at one pile of elephant dung). The dung beetle belongs to a varied subfamily of about 4 500 species worldwide, 800 of which occur in southern Africa. An individual of the *Scaraboeus*

ABOVE Thousands of dung beetles – the 'vacuum cleaners of the veld' – gather within moments around fresh elephant droppings.

group, perhaps the most familiar, puts together a ball of dung up to 40 times its own weight and, using its back legs as propellants, rolls it away for burial. Male and female then prepare a small part of it as a 'brood' (egg-protecting) ball.

These beetles do much for the general health of the environment, helping to destroy bacterial and other disease vectors and parasites that, left alone, would find their way into the intestines of herbivores. And by carrying away the dung they return precious, nurturing nitrogen to the soil.

Spiders are everywhere, of course, notable for their variety as well as their numbers. Some have unusual working lives, 'fishing', for example, in the placid waters of wetlands, others 'flying' at immense heights and for immense distances on silken threads. The wolf spider navigates by the position of the sun. There are trapdoor spiders, stalkers-and-pouncers, chasers, jumpers, web-spinners, ambushers. Among the especially eye-catching sights are the multi-hued webs of the orb-spinners of the genus *Nepila* – enormous golden webs erected between the trees. Then there are the baboon spiders, also noticeable. Indeed they can hardly be missed when they do appear: they are large, long-limbed and hairy, and will rear up with their front legs outstretched when threatened – a fearsome spectacle, but in fact the creature is relatively harmless. Perhaps the most intriguing of southern African species is the bolus spider, which produces a strong thread of silk with a ball of glue at the end, lures its prey by emitting

a false pheromone, whirls the bolus around rather in the manner of a hammer thrower in an athletics arena, and hurls it to ensnare the victim.

Of all the Lowveld's tree species, the baobab is perhaps the strangest. Huge, long-lived, with a thick grey trunk and absurdly spindly branches, it is the very stuff of local legend and myth. Some folk believe that the Creator planted it upside down, others that its blossoms are the home of spirits, still others that a beverage distilled from the seeds will protect you from crocodiles. Many baobabs are immensely old, some of them starting their lives well before the birth of the Roman Empire, and they grow to gigantic proportions. Indeed one hollowed-out specimen near the Murchison range to the west served the early gold miners as a pub.

The tree, though, has other and perhaps more sensible uses: the fruits contain tartaric and vitamin C-rich ascorbic acid, potassium bitartrate (perhaps more commonly known as 'cream of tartar') which, in solution, makes a rather nice drink; the leaves an edible vegetable; the seeds a palatable coffee substitute.

Appearances, though, are deceptive. This solid-looking giant is in fact little more than a mass of soft wood fibre and water and, for all the centuries it has weathered, its end is quick and catastrophic. The tree may die of disease or have absorbed too much rainwater, but, whatever the final blow, it dies suddenly, the great structure collapsing in moments to leave a barely noticeable pile of vegetable matter to mark its once majestic presence.

ABOVE The dusk light of sunset illuminates the waters of the Letaba River. The bushveld's riverine plant life is dense and varied, graced by mahogany and nyala trees, huge sycamore figs and, in the north, ghostly fever trees.

BELOW The great and gilded home of the golden orb-web spider, spun between adjacent trees or bushes and strong enough to snare birds. The spiders themselves are variously and brightly coloured, and although timid and barely venomous, they can inflict a sharp bite. This, however, is a rare event.

OPPOSITE An ancient baobab stands sentinel over the twilit reaches of the northern Kruger National Park. The trees are the subject of much myth and legend; the facts are almost as intriguing as the fiction (see page 95).

OPPOSITE, TOP LEFT The African (or weeping) wattle is a bushveld tree that attracts sap-sucking insects that excrete water, hence the alternative name.

OPPOSITE, TOP RIGHT The delicate, brightly coloured blooms of the impala lily.

OPPOSITE, BOTTOM LEFT The bark and fruit of the sausage tree are used in traditional medicine, though with caution: the former is toxic.

OPPOSITE, BOTTOM RIGHT The sickle-bush is an untidy small tree that tends to be invasive. The pods are eaten by some mammals.

ABOVE LEFT The mopane pomegranate covers much of the bushveld region.

ABOVE CENTRE The sjambok pod is often associated with termite mounds. A drink made from the roots is said to be an effective cure for blackwater fever.

ABOVE RIGHT The dwarf boer-bean grows along the Lebombo mountains to the east. The flowers are rich in nectar, attracting an array of birds.

RIGHT Some members of the huge acacia family have deadly thorns. Parts of the bushveld are in fact known as thornveld; among the region's prominent species are knobthorn, umbrella thorn and redthorn.

Prince of Parks

Wherever wildlife conservation is discussed, not only in Africa but around the world, the Kruger National Park is invariably cited as a pathfinder in the field. This magnificent sanctuary covers most of South Africa's Lowveld plain – some 20 000 square kilometres (7 720 square miles) of heat-hazed savanna and woodland that stretches from the Crocodile River in the south to Kipling's great and grey Limpopo in the north (though the river is rather greater in fiction than in fact).

Broadly speaking, Kruger can be divided according to its vegetation types. South of the Olifants River, which more or less cuts the park in half, you will find acacia, red bushwillow and combretum, the eastern parts graced by pastures of buffalo and red grasses shaded by hardy knobthorn trees. The countryside to the north of the Olifants is covered largely by mopane, a tree or shrub with dark-red wood and leaves that are shaped like butterflies on the wing, and which smell vaguely of turpentine.

ABOVE Neat picnic stopovers are scattered throughout the park, and are among the few places where you are allowed to leave your vehicle.

ABOVE Lazing leopard. The Kruger National Park is sanctuary to about a thousand of these handsome and powerful big cats. Lucky is the visitor who manages to spot one – these are nocturnal animals, and masters of camouflage.

Plant life changes again as you reach the far north. This is a unique and, in geophysical terms, quite remarkable region, the meeting place of no fewer than nine of Africa's major ecosystems. Among other elements, it embraces bushveld and grassy plain, woodland and deep-green forest, wetland, sandveld, granite hill and lava flat, a land of striking contrasts, the diversity of landscape and flora complemented by a variety of trees and shrubs, reptiles, birds, insects. Many of the life forms are found in few other places, a few nowhere else in the world. Of special note are the Lebombo ironwoods, ebonies and mahoganies, the great baobabs of the Mashikiri, the phantom-like fever trees standing pale along the silent reaches of the Luvuvhu River, and the teeming wildlife of the Hlamalala plain.

Kruger is home, of course, to the Big Five animals – lion and leopard, rhino, elephant and buffalo – but also to more than 40 other mammal species. Of these, lions are the game-viewer's prime quarry, and the big cats are numerous enough, and feel secure enough, to be fairly visible. You can probably count on seeing at least one pride during the first couple of days of your stay. Elephant and buffalo are even more prominent, rhino much less so, and you will be very lucky if you manage to spot the solitary and elusive leopard.

Stayover visitors base themselves at one or another of 20 or so rest camps, 12 of which are largish clusters of family bungalows, cottages, huts, guesthouses and caravan-camping sites and, many of them, with their own, much smaller and less well-appointed satellite encampments. Also on offer are half a dozen attractive, rather isolated bushveld camps with limited facilities but plenty of privacy and loads of character, each holding the promise of an intimate experience with the 'real' Africa. Accommodation options also include tented camps, bush lodges and private safari camps, the last two at the more luxurious end of the scale.

The public rest camps are pleasant, unpretentious places, fenced against wild animals (most usefully pilfering against

ABOVE At Kruger's secluded, somewhat remote bushveld camps facilities may be fairly modest, but the experience unforgettable.

baboons and hyaenas), neatly laid out and embowered by indigenous trees. The chalets and bungalows are spacious and comfortable; an average family unit will have two two-bed

ABOVE Small herds of elephant are a common sight on safari in southern Africa and are among the stars of the show.

rooms, a bathroom, a kitchen equipped with stove, fridge, utensils and tableware, a mosquito-proof veranda, and an outside barbecue area that beckons when the sky is brilliant with stars and the night-time sounds of wild Africa fill the air.

Routines are undemanding, the emphasis on informality and affordable outdoor living. Each camp has its restaurant, though many guests prefer to look after themselves: the camp shop stocks meat, groceries, dry goods, alcohol, magazines and oddments. Most people, too, explore Kruger on self-drive excursions, making their way along part of the 2 700-kilometre network of fully surfaced or good gravel roads to the water holes, viewing points and picnic spots. On some stretches the wildlife is prolific, the landscapes the kind of raw wilderness that will stir the senses and live long in the memory.

Nearly all the camps are strategically sited near a river or beside a water hole. Letaba, for example, is a handsome collection of buildings set above a sweeping bend in the Letaba River, and its terraces are ideal for game-viewing, the grounds enhanced by trim lawns, aloes, flowering shrubs, ilala palms and mahogany trees. It is also well positioned, at the junction of three routes, for game drives to the north, west and south. Even more magnificently situated is the Olifants rest camp, which perches a hundred and more metres above the river of that name, offering spectacular views down to the lush, game-rich valley below and to the distant hills beyond. The vista is memorable in all seasons and at all times, but especially at dawn and sunset.

Perhaps the place with the most charm is Punda Maria, way up in the north and one of the oldest camps (it was named after the wife of an early ranger). It is quite small, tucked away among rocky hills and groves of evergreen trees, popular for its laid-back, sociable atmosphere and for its proximity to an especially fascinating area rich both in its wildlife and its scenery. By contrast, Berg-en-Dal ('Hill-and-Valley') and Mopani are newish camps, both intelligently conceived to blend with their wilderness environments.

Largest and liveliest of the camps, is Skukuza, a place with all the amenities typical of a small urban centre. The focal point of Skukuza is the reception and restaurant area, said to be the largest thatched building in Africa and perhaps even the world.

The great majority of Kruger visitors explore the park in the comfort of their own air-conditioned vehicles, but for those with energy, time to spare and a compulsion to get closer to the wilderness there is a range of walking trails from which to choose, foot safaris led by guides who know the lore of the wild and are willing to share their knowledge. The walks are not especially challenging, and certainly not competitive – they are designed simply to stimulate the mind and eye, meandering, go-where-you-will excursions that lead wherever the mood and interest of the group dictate. One stops now and again along the route to examine an insect, a tree, a bird's nest, a herd of antelope, and in the evening to cook supper, socialise and, finally, bed down. Camp sites and huts can be somewhat basic but comfortable enough – and companionable. On these hikes, one meets acquaintances who soon become and often remain good friends.

ABOVE Negotiating Kruger's Lebombo auto trail. Drives should be leisurely – the world of wildlife cannot be enjoyed by rushing.

LEFT The still waters of a dam near the Bateleur rest camp, set on the bank of the often dry Shingwedzi River in the northern part of the Kruger National Park. Bateleur boasts a splendid viewing platform overlooking a permanent pool.

ABOVE Game-viewing at one of Kruger's dams. These resources do much to cushion the effects of periodical droughts. The animals tend to congregate at these times, and the dams then become prime wildlife-watching venues.

OPPOSITE The Lebombo mountains eco-trail makes its way along the game-rich eastern areas of the Kruger National Park.

ABOVE A boulder-strewn outcrop in the Shilowa area of the Kruger National Park. Mammals often seen in these rugged areas include the agile little klipspringer – but not when a rock-loving leopard is also in residence.

OPPOSITE An ancient nyala tree adds a little shade to the heat-seared bushveld in Kruger's north-central region. Nyalas are often found growing on large anthills; their fruit is edible, either fresh or ground up to make a kind of flour.

TOP LEFT Among Kruger venues is the Stevenson-Hamilton memorial and its rugged setting. The man commemorated was the ruthless conservationist who looked after the sanctuary, then known as the Sabie, in its infancy.

TOP RIGHT The popular Bateleur bushveld camp is cosy, comfortable, rather isolated, and beautifully embowered.

LEFT The traditional craft centre at Kruger's Numbi Gate, in the southern part of the park, features wood carvings and basketwork.

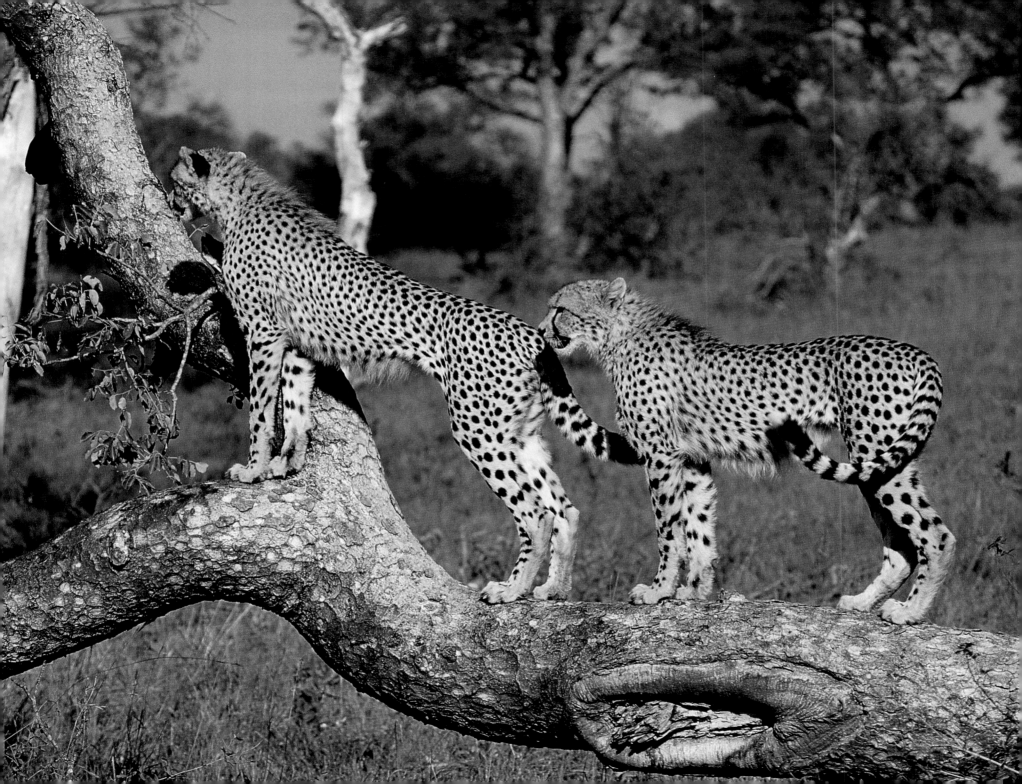